THE BEATITU
6 STUDIES FOR GROUP

CW00689669

MEEKNESS

Claiming your Inheritance

James & Carol Plueddemann

ZondervanPublishingHouse
Grand Rapids, Michigan

A Division of HarperCollins*Publishers*

MEEKNESS: CLAIMING YOUR INHERITANCE
Copyright © 1993 by Jim & Carol Plueddemann
All rights reserved

Requests for information should be addressed to:
Zondervan Publishing House
Grand Rapids, MI 49530

ISBN 0-310-59623-8

Edited by Jack Kuhatschek
Cover design by John M. Lucas
Cover illustration by George Disario
Interior design by Louise Bauer

Printed in the United States of America

93 94 95 96 97 98 / ❖ DP / 10 9 8 7 6 5 4 3 2 1

Contents

The Beatitude Series

Welcome to the Beatitude Series. This series is designed to help you develop the eight character qualities found in those whom Jesus calls "blessed."

The Beatitudes are among the best-known and best-loved words of Jesus. They form the heart of the Sermon on the Mount, found in Matthew 5–7 and Luke 6:17–49. In eight brief statements Jesus describes the lifestyle that God desires and rewards:

> *Blessed are the poor in spirit,*
>   *for theirs is the kingdom of heaven.*
> *Blessed are those who mourn,*
>   *for they will be comforted.*
> *Blessed are the meek,*
>   *for they will inherit the earth.*
> *Blessed are those who hunger and thirst for righteousness,*
>   *for they will be filled.*
> *Blessed are the merciful,*
>   *for they will be shown mercy.*
> *Blessed are the pure in heart,*
>   *for they will see God.*
> *Blessed are the peacemakers,*
>   *for they will be called sons of God.*
> *Blessed are those who are persecuted because of righteousness,*
>   *for theirs is the kingdom of heaven.*

The Beatitudes turn the world's values upside down. We are tempted to say: "*Wretched* are the poor, for they have so little money. *Wretched* are those who mourn, for no one will hear their cries. *Wretched* are the meek, for they will be trampled by the powerful." Yet Jesus shatters our stereotypes and asserts that the poor will be rich, the mourners will be comforted, and the meek will inherit everything. What a strange kingdom he offers!

In recent years there has been some confusion about the kind of blessing Christ promises in these verses. The Beatitudes have been described as "God's prescription for happiness." One book has even called them "The Be-Happy Attitudes."

The Greek word *makarios* can mean "happy." J. B. Phillips translates the opening words of each beatitude, "How happy are . . . !" Nevertheless, John Stott writes:

> It is seriously misleading to render *makarios* "happy." For happiness is a subjective state, whereas Jesus is making an objective judgment about these people. He is declaring not what they may feel like ("happy"), but what God thinks of them and what on that account they are: they are "blessed".[1]

The eight guides in the Beatitude Series give you an in-depth look at each beatitude. But Jesus is not describing eight different types of people—some who are meek, others who are merciful, and still others who are peacemakers. He desires to see all eight character qualities in every one of his followers.

That's a tall order! Only those who enter Christ's kingdom by faith can expect such a transformation. And only those who serve the King can enjoy his rewards.

Our prayer is that The Beatitude Series will give you a clearer and deeper grasp of what it truly means to be blessed.

HOW TO USE THE BEATITUDE SERIES

The Beatitude Series is designed to be flexible. You can use the guides in any order that is best for you or your group. They are ideal for Sunday-school classes, small groups, one-on-one relationships, or as materials for your quiet times.

Because each guide contains only six studies, you can easily explore more than one beatitude. In a Sunday-school class, any two guides can be combined for a quarter (twelve weeks), or the entire series can be covered in a year.

Each study deliberately focuses on a limited number of passages, usually only one or two. That allows you to see each passage in its context, avoiding the temptation of prooftexting and the frustration of "Bible hopscotch" (jumping from verse to verse). If you would like to look up additional passages, a Bible concordance will give the most help.

The Beatitude Series helps you *discover* what the Bible says rather than simply *telling* you the answers. The questions encourage you to think and to explore options rather than merely to fill in the blanks with one-word answers.

Leader's notes are provided in the back of each guide. They show how to lead a group discussion, provide additional information on questions, and suggest ways to deal with problems that may come up in the discussion. With such helps, someone with little or no experience can lead an effective study.

SUGGESTIONS FOR INDIVIDUAL STUDY

1. Begin each study with prayer. Ask God to help you understand the passage and to apply it to your life.

2. A good modern translation, such as the *New International Version,* the *New American Standard Bible,* or the *New Revised Standard Version,* will give you the most help. Questions in this guide, however, are based on the *New International Version.*

3. Read and reread the passage(s). You must know what the passage says before you can understand what it means and how it applies to you.

4. Write your answers in the space provided in the study guide. This will help you to clearly express your understanding of the passage.

5. Keep a Bible dictionary handy. Use it to look up any unfamiliar words, names, or places.

SUGGESTIONS FOR GROUP STUDY

1. Come to the study prepared. Careful preparation will greatly enrich your time in group discussion.

2. Be willing to join in the discussion. The leader of the group will not be lecturing but will encourage people to discuss what they have learned in the passage. Plan to share what God has taught you in your individual study.

3. Stick to the passage being studied. Base your answers on the verses being discussed rather than on outside authorities such as commentaries or your favorite author or speaker.

4. Try to be sensitive to the other members of the group. Listen attentively when they speak, and be affirming whenever you can. This will encourage more hesitant members of the group to participate.

5. Be careful not to dominate the discussion. By all means participate! But allow others to have equal time.

6. If you are the discussion leader, you will find additional suggestions and helpful ideas in the leader's notes at the back of the guide.

Note

1. *The Message of the Sermon on the Mount* (Downers Grove, Ill.: InterVarsity Press, 1978), 33.

Introducing Meekness

Blessed are the meek,
for they will inherit the earth.

Meekness? Who wants to be meek? We live in a world that worships *power!* Paul Tournier writes:

> Power has become the supreme value, the only one that is universally recognized—all kinds of power: military, political, economic, industrial; the power of technology . . . the power of the masses, of sexual desires; the power of youth, of muscular strength and records counted in hundredths of a second; the power of money and of wealth.[1]

Books like *Looking Out for No. 1* and *Winning Through Intimidation* have become best-sellers. People flock to assertiveness-training sessions and seminars to help us "unleash the power within us," but when was the last time you heard about a workshop on meekness?

In many people's minds, meekness and weakness are synonymous—they even rhyme! We tend to think of a meek person as a wimp, someone who allows everyone to push him around. Actually, true meekness requires unusual strength. It is particularly challenging because it is so foreign to contemporary thinking.

The Greek word for "meek" means "gentle," "humble," "considerate," "courteous," and "therefore exercising the self-control without which these qualities would be impossible."[2] D. Martyn Lloyd-Jones writes that "meekness is essentially a true view of oneself, expressing itself in attitude and conduct with respect to others. . . . The man who is truly meek is the one who is truly amazed that God and man can think of him as well as they do and treat him as well as they do."[3] Because those who are meek have a biblical view of themselves, they treat others with gentleness, humility, and patience.

Jesus promises that the meek "will inherit the earth." That is the opposite of what we would expect. In this life those who are aggressive and powerful often trample the meek, leaving them empty-handed. But when Jesus returns to establish his upside-down kingdom, the mourners will laugh, the hungry will be filled, and the meek will possess everything.

Meekness is a quality of God's kingdom people. Once we understand how radical Jesus' call to meekness is, we may be tempted to dismiss it as impossible. But we have supernatural resources and strong examples to follow. And the rewards are eternal! Join us in exploring what it means to live in God's kingdom of radical reversal and surprising joy.

Jim & Carol Plueddemann

Notes

1. Quoted by David Prior, *Jesus and Power* (Downers Grove, Ill.: InterVarsity Press, 1987).

2. John R. W. Stott, *The Message of the Sermon on the Mount* (Downers Grove, Ill.: InterVarsity Press, 1978), p. 42.

3. Quoted in Stott, *Sermon on the Mount*, p. 43.

The Dangers of Pride

DANIEL 4

Did you ever play "King of the Mountain" when you were growing up? Remember the sense of power you had when you were at the top of the hill? And the dejection you felt when you found yourself at the bottom?

King Nebuchadnezzar was one of the most powerful of the Babylonian kings. He became extremely proud of his accomplishments and of his great empire. But when he conquered the little nation of Judah, he was introduced to the God of the Jews—a God who demanded exclusive worship. God literally brought Nebuchadnezzar to the ground until he recognized who was really in control of nations and kings. The great conqueror was himself conquered by his Creator. Nebuchadnezzar's experience can help us understand the dangers of pride and the blessings of meekness.

1. Has there been a time in your life when you felt like you were "on top of the world" but then found yourself "eating dust"? What caused the change?

2. Read Daniel 4:1 – 27. What does Nebuchadnezzar's dream reveal about his prosperity and success?

3. Why do you think Daniel was "perplexed" and "terrified" by the king's dream (v. 19)?

4. What impresses you about the way Daniel breaks the news of the dream's meaning to the king?

5. What hopeful sign did the gloomy dream include?

6. What did Nebuchadnezzar need to learn about himself and about "the Most High God" (vv. 17, 25, 26)?

In what other ways did his life need to change (v. 27)?

7. Why can an inadequate view of God lead to an inflated view of ourselves?

Why does pride have a negative effect on our lifestyle?

8. Read Daniel 4:28–37. Why do you think Nebuchadnezzar failed to respond to God's warning (vv. 28–30)?

9. How did Nebuchadnezzer's humiliating experience change his attitude toward God?

10. What does Nebuchadnezzar's story say to you about the destructive dangers of pride?

11. Pride is not always as obvious as it was in Nebuchadnezzar's life. What are some of the more subtle ways pride can show up in our lives?

12. What experiences has God used in your life to remind you that "Heaven rules" (v. 26)?

BETWEEN STUDIES

Reflect this week on the differences between selfish ambition and godly ambition. When is ambition a positive characteristic? When is it destructive?

Write out Matthew 6:33 on a 3 x 5 card and put it where you can see it often. Pray for godly ambition this week—ambition for God's kingdom rule in your life.

The Meekness of Christ

PHILIPPIANS 2:1–18

The buzz-words for success in today's competitive world are *assertiveness, empowerment,* and *self-generated fulfillment.* From cradle to grave, we are urged to feel good and to reach our full potential.

God's model for success offers an astounding contrast to all that we hear around us. Self-renunciation, humility, and gentleness are the keys for success in God's "upside-down" kingdom. His definition of power requires meekness, not might.

How can we begin to grasp this radically different concept? We need a role-model to show us what meekness looks like. And we have that in Jesus himself.

1. In what situations are you most likely to assert yourself and stand up for your own rights?

2. Read Philippians 2:1–4. What hints in these verses indicate that a "me-first" mindset isn't a new, 20th-century problem?

3. What four motives for living in unity does Paul give (v. 1)?

4. What spiritual resources for this kind of unity do you see in verse 1?

5. What is the difference between true humility and putting yourself down?

6. Read Philippians 2:5–11. Verses 6–11 are probably an early church hymn. In what specific ways did Jesus make himself "nothing" and "humble himself"?

7. How do each of Jesus' actions illustrate the attitude Paul described in verses 3–4?

8. How might this attitude affect your relationships in your family or at work?

9. What difference would you see in your church if each person adopted this attitude?

10. Read Philippians 2:12–18. In light of the chapter so far, what might Paul mean when he says "work out your salvation" (v. 12)?

What is God's part in your salvation? What is your part?

11. What characteristics make God's children "shine like stars"?

12. Pray about the challenge of shining through the darkness of sin in your world this week.

BETWEEN STUDIES

Analyze the TV and magazine ads you see this week, specifically looking for media messages about what it means to be a successful and powerful person. Then contrast these messages with the model of Philippians 2.

If you are in a study group, share your observations with them next week.

3

Meekness in Action

MARK 10:32–45; JOHN 13:1–17

George Whitefield, a twenty-two-year-old preacher in London, prayed, "O Heavenly Father, for Thy dear Son's sake, keep me from climbing." Whitefield was the boy wonder of London. Great crowds came to hear him preach and hundreds were converted to faith in Christ. Eventually he crossed the Atlantic thirteen times, ministering extensively in America as well as Great Britain. He had a lifelong practice of reading the Scriptures on his knees.

Whitefield was a contemporary of John and Charles Wesley and helped to found the Methodist church. But he handed over leadership of the movement to the Wesleys saying, "I think it my highest privilege to be an assistant to all but the head of none."

Most people today are grabbing for power and influence. What did Jesus think of power? How did he use it? These passages in Mark and John help us see true meekness in action.

1. What did your parents want you to be when you grew up? What did you want to be?

2. Read Mark 10:32–45. Why were Jesus' followers astonished and afraid about going to Jerusalem?

3. In light of what Jesus told his disciples in verses 32–34, how do you think he felt about their request (vv. 35–37)?

4. What were James and John still failing to understand about Jesus' kingdom?

5. Why is it so hard for us to grasp that this is the age of suffering, not glory (see also Rom. 8:18; 2 Cor. 4:17)?

6. What do you think Jesus meant by his "cup" and his "baptism" (vv. 38–40)?

7. What did the response of the other ten disciples indicate about their attitudes (v. 41)?

8. How did Jesus use this tense situation to teach new insights about leadership?

How does his teaching contrast with popular views of leadership—both then and now?

9. How would Jesus show ultimate servanthood in the future (v. 45)?

10. Read John 13:1–17. What did Jesus know that his disciples failed to grasp (vv. 1, 3, 11)?

How does this knowledge add to the significance of Jesus' actions?

11. What did Peter fail to realize about being washed by Jesus that he would understand later (vv. 6–11)?

12. What does Jesus want us to learn from his example (vv. 12–17)?

13. Who, in your experience, has best shown you what it means to "wash feet" and be a servant leader?

14. What would it mean for you to practice footwashing in your various relationships?

BETWEEN STUDIES

Plan a specific way to serve someone this week in a way that goes beyond your normal actions.

If you are in a study group, you might also plan to do a service project together. Plan for this prayerfully and spend time afterwards reflecting together on what this experience meant to you.

4

Meekness Is Not Weakness

2 CORINTHIANS 10:1–11; 12:7–10

Have you ever studied charts that categorize human temperaments? The classic categories are choleric, sanguine, phlegmatic, and melancholic. Choleric personalities are the strong, quick-tempered, leader types. Sanguines are outgoing, confident optimists. Phlegmatics tend to be calm, cool, and easygoing. Melancholic personalities are sensitive and reflective.

Of course, people are really too complex to be categorized, but differences in temperament are obvious and quite fascinating. At first glance, we might expect that meekness would come easier to phlegmatics and melancholics. But *all* Christians are called to be meek—whatever their temperaments. Meekness doesn't come naturally; it's a supernatural characteristic produced by the Spirit of God.

The apostle Paul was a strong, choleric personality who didn't shy away from confrontation. He showed that meekness and strength are compatible. In fact, meekness is really power—

power under control. As you look at 2 Corinthians 10, you might be surprised by what Paul says about meekness.

1. When you think of someone who is "meek," what images come to mind?

2. Read 2 Corinthians 10:1–11. Though the majority of believers in Corinth sided with Paul, a vocal minority slandered him and questioned his authority. What were some of the things they were saying about him (vv. 1–2, 10)?

3. Paul appeals to his critics "by the meekness and gentleness of Christ" (v. 1). How was this a subtle rebuke to those who viewed Paul's meekness as weakness?

4. What did those who looked "only on the surface" (v. 7) misunderstand about Paul's weapons and warfare (vv. 3–6)?

5. In what ways are we guilty today of using worldly weapons to fight spiritual battles?

What spiritual weapons do we have in our arsenal?

6. What does Paul see as the purpose for his authority (v. 8)?

7. What examples have you seen of Christians who use their authority to build people up? To pull people down?

8. How can you demonstrate Christ's meekness and gentleness in your leadership roles at home, in your workplace, and in your church?

9. Read 2 Corinthians 12:7–10. Why did God give Paul a thorn in the flesh?

10. What does this account show about the value God places on humility?

11. Paul gives an interesting equation here: weakness = power. How does he explain this?

12. When have you seen God use weakness to show his strength?

13. What steps do you need to take to cultivate powerful meekness in your life?

BETWEEN STUDIES

Under two columns, write down your strengths and weaknesses. How might your strengths also be weaknesses? And how might God use your weaknesses as strengths?

To get a clearer perspective, reflect on your strengths and weaknesses with someone who knows you well. Pray together for true humility to accept yourself as the person God made you, recognizing that all your gifts are from him.

My Strengths	My Weaknesses

Meekness in Ministry

2 TIMOTHY 2:22–26; 1 PETER 5:1–11

Believe it or not, cruel Nero was known for his *kindness* before he became the ruler of Rome. But after he assumed power, he became a tyrant. He drove wildly through the streets of Rome, running over anyone who got in his way, and he lit his garden at night with the burning bodies of saints.

Leadership can be dangerous! Whenever we are put in a position of influence over others, we are tempted to control, manipulate, and lust for more power. Leadership is the acid test for meekness and gentleness.

Every Christian has opportunities to lead and influence others. In this study we'll explore why meekness is a vital part of our ministry.

1. Who has been the most influential and godly leader in your life? What made this person a good leader?

28

2. Read 2 Timothy 2:22–26. Running away is usually considered cowardly. When might it be the best and most effective strategy?

3. In contrast to fleeing, what goals does Paul tell Timothy to *pursue?*

In what ways can you actively pursue these things?

4. What character qualities does Paul outline for God's servants?

5. Why is meekness (gentleness, humility) so important in Paul's job description?

6. How much emphasis do you think meekness gets in the typical job description for Christian leaders today? Explain.

7. Read 1 Peter 5:1–11. What future hope does Peter look forward to (vv. 1, 4, and 10)?

8. Meanwhile, what qualities does he encourage the "shepherds of God's flock" to cultivate?

9. What good and bad motives for ministry are given here?

What examples have you seen of these positive and negative motives?

10. What grade would you give yourself on Peter's test for effective ministry? Explain.

11. In what ways do you need to "clothe yourself with humility" during the coming week?

12. What promises of comfort and strength can you take from this passage for your life and your ministry?

BETWEEN STUDIES

Reflect prayerfully on the ministry opportunities you have this week. In the chart below, list each opportunity you have and ask God to give you the strength of meekness in all your relationships.

Study Luke 22:24–27 and pray that you will resist the temptation to "lord it over" anyone under your care.

Ministry Opportunities This Week

6

The Meek Will Inherit

PSALM 37:1–11

"Truck-driver Inherits Fortune from Unknown Relative."

We've all heard stories of people who found themselves suddenly rich because they received an inheritance or discovered oil in their back yard. But did you ever hear of someone becoming rich by being meek?

When Jesus said, "Blessed are the meek, for they will inherit the earth," he was quoting Psalm 37, today's passage. What did Jesus mean, and what did the psalmist mean? This study will help you find out.

1. Why do you think that evil sometimes leads to prosperity while doing good results in suffering?

2. Read Psalm 37:1–11. According to the psalmist, how are we tempted to respond when evil people prosper (vv. 1, 7–8)?

Why do you think we are inclined to respond that way?

3. In contrast to our natural tendency, what positive responses does the psalmist command (vv. 1, 3–5, 7–9)?

4. What specific promises are we given if we obey these commands?

5. Do you think this psalm supports "prosperity theology"— the teaching that Christianity will make you healthy and wealthy? Why or why not?

6. Do not fret! The psalmist repeats this advice three times (vv. 1, 7, 8). What are some of the fretful situations in your life right now?

What would it take to commit these situations to the Lord?

7. How does worry reveal a lack of trust?

8. What connection is there between worry, trust, and meekness?

9. From a human standpoint, why is it surprising that the meek will inherit the earth?

10. In your life, what might it mean to make "your righteousness shine like the dawn" (v. 6)?

BETWEEN STUDIES

When Alexander Solzhenitsyn was in prison in Russia he came to realize that

> as long as he was trying to maintain some power—whether it was for food, clothing, or health—he was at the mercy of his captors. When he realized and accepted, and even embraced his powerlessness, then he became completely free; the power of his captors over him ceased. In the way of life's strange paradoxes, he became the powerful, they the powerless (Richard Foster, *Money, Sex, and Power* [London: Hodder & Stoughton, 1985], 205).

Make a list of the commands in Psalm 37:1–8. Beside each command, make a note of how you will carry it out in your life this week. Ask one person to pray for you regularly as you make these qualities a part of your life.

Leader's Notes

Leading a Bible discussion—especially for the first time—can make you feel both nervous and excited. If you are nervous, realize that you are in good company. Many biblical leaders, such as Moses, Joshua, and the apostle Paul, felt nervous and inadequate to lead others (see, for example, 1 Corinthians 2:3). Yet God's grace was sufficient for them, just as it will be for you.

Some excitement is also natural. Your leadership is a gift to the others in the group. Keep in mind, however, that other group members also share responsibility for the group. Your role is simply to stimulate discussion by asking questions and encouraging people to respond. The suggestions listed below can help you to be an effective leader.

PREPARING TO LEAD

1. Ask God to help you understand and apply the passage to your own life. Unless that happens, you will not be prepared to lead others.

2. Carefully work through each question in the study guide. Meditate and reflect on the passage as you formulate your answers.

3. Familiarize yourself with the leader's notes for the study. These will help you understand the purpose of the study and will provide valuable information about the questions in the study.

4. Pray for the various members of the group. Ask God to use these studies to make you better disciples of Jesus Christ.

5. Before the first meeting, make sure each person has a study guide. Encourage them to prepare beforehand for each study.

LEADING THE STUDY

1. Begin the study on time. If people realize that the study begins on schedule, they will work harder to arrive on time.

2. At the beginning of your first time together, explain that these studies are designed to be discussions, not lectures. Encourage everyone to participate, but realize that some may be hesitant to speak during the first few sessions.

3. Read the introductory paragraph at the beginning of the discussion. This will orient the group to the passage being studied.

4. Read the passage aloud. You may choose to do this yourself, or you might ask for volunteers.

5. The questions in the guide are designed to be used just as they are written. If you wish, you may simply read each one aloud to the group. Or you may prefer to express them in your own words. Unnecessary rewording of the questions, however, is not recommended.

6. Don't be afraid of silence. People in the group may need time to think before responding.

7. Avoid answering your own questions. If necessary, rephrase a question until it is clearly understood. Even an eager group will quickly become passive and silent if they think the leader will do most of the talking.

8. Encourage more than one answer to each question. Ask, "What do the rest of you think?" or "Anyone else?" until several people have had a chance to respond.

9. Try to be affirming whenever possible. Let people know you appreciate their insights into the passage.

10. Never reject an answer. If it is clearly wrong, ask, "Which verse led you to that conclusion?" Or let the group handle the problem by asking them what they think about the question.

11. Avoid going off on tangents. If people wander off course, gently bring them back to the passage being considered.

12. Conclude your time together with conversational prayer. Ask God to help you apply those things that you learned in the study.

13. End on time. This will be easier if you control the pace of the discussion by not spending too much time on some questions or too little on others.

Many more suggestions and helps are found in the book *Leading Bible Discussions* (InterVarsity Press). Reading it would be well worth your time.

STUDY 1
The Dangers of Pride
DANIEL 4

Purpose: To replace pride in our lives with godly ambition.

Question 1 Every study begins with an "approach question," which is discussed *before* reading the passage. An approach question is designed to do three things.

First, it helps to break the ice. Because an approach question doesn't require any knowledge of the passage or any special preparation, it can get people talking and can help them to warm up to each other.

Second, an approach question can motivate people to study the passage at hand. At the beginning of the study, people in the group aren't necessarily ready to jump into the world of the Bible. Their minds may be on other things (their kids, a problem at work, an upcoming meeting) that have nothing to do with the study. An approach question can capture their interest and draw them into the discussion by raising important issues related to the study. The question becomes a bridge between their personal lives and the answers found in Scripture.

Third, a good approach question can reveal where people's thoughts or feelings need to be transformed by Scripture. That is why it is important to ask the approach question *before* reading the passage. The passage might inhibit the spontaneous, honest answers people might have given, because they feel compelled to give biblical answers. The approach question allows them to compare their personal thoughts and feelings with what they later discover in Scripture.

Question 2 Note verses 4, 10–12, 20–22, and 27.

Question 3 It took great courage for Daniel to tell the king that he would become a wild animal! Daniel had been under threat of death from the king before (Dan. 2:13), and he knew what kind of power Nebuchadnezzar had.

Question 4 "Daniel must have been severely tempted to hide something of the severest aspect of the word. In his sympathy he uttered his wish that the curse of the dream might have fallen on others and not on the king (verse 19). But he knew that only words of brutal frankness could have the strength to avert the coming calamity. There could be no cheap and immediate comfort for the man before him at this time, and no impression must be left on him that such was possible" (Ronald S. Wallace, *The Lord Is King: The Message of Daniel* [Downers Grove, Ill.: InterVarsity Press, 1979], p. 81).

Question 6 Proud Nebuchadnezzar needed to learn that his prosperity and success were a gift from God. They were not the result of his "mighty power and . . . majesty" (v. 30). Notice the expression "the lowliest of men" (v. 17)—a phrase designed to humble Nebuchadnezzar and put him in his place.

Question 7 Of course, the opposite is true as well. An inadequate view of God can lead to a low view of our value and worth. But the focus of Daniel 4 is on pride, so don't get side-tracked on discussions about low self-esteem.

Question 8 Notice that the king had twelve full months between the time of the warning and the fulfillment of the dream (v. 29).

"The 'seven times' [mentioned in verses 23, 25, and 32] were probably seven years because a) seven days or months would have been inadequate for his hair to have grown to the length of feathers (v. 33), and b) 'times' in 7:25 means years" (John F. Walvoord and Roy B. Zuck, *Bible Knowledge Commentary* [Wheaton, Ill.: Victor Books, 1985], p. 1342).

STUDY 2
Meekness of Christ
PHILIPPIANS 2:1–18

Purpose: To understand what meekness meant in Jesus' life and to adopt the same attitude in our relationships.

Question 2 Apparently there was a double threat to the unity of the Philippian church: there were false teachers coming in from outside (3:1–3) and disagreeing members from within (4:1–3).

Question 4 The unity Paul is appealing for requires supernatural help. Verse 1 explains that God's people are "united with Christ." This intimate relationship with Christ is the basis for being united with other believers and provides "comfort from his love." In addition, believers have "fellowship with the Spirit," another powerful resource for living in unity.

Question 6 "Christ did not empty himself of the form of God (i.e., his deity), but of the manner of existence as equal to God. He did not lay aside the divine attributes, but 'the insignia of majesty' (Lightfoot, p. 112). Mark Twain's novel *The Prince and the Pauper,* describing a son of Henry VIII who temporarily changed positions with a poor boy in London, provides an illustration. . . .

After describing the fact of the Incarnation, Paul turns to the consideration of the depths of humiliation to which Christ went: 'he humbled himself' and went to 'death on a cross.'. . . The opening phrase of 2:8 looks at him from the standpoint of how he appeared in the estimation of men. He was 'found' by them, as far as his external appearance was concerned, as a mere man. Outwardly considered, he was no different from other men. Even this was great condescension for one who possessed the form of God, but Christ's incomparable act did not end here. He further humbled himself by 'becoming obedient to death.' He was so committed to the Father's plan that he obeyed it even as far as death (Heb 5:8). Nor was this all, for it was no ordinary death, but the disgraceful death by crucifixion, a death not allowed for Roman citizens, and to Jews indicative of the curse of God" (Homer A. Kent, Jr., *Philippians,* The Expositor's Bible Commentary [Grand Rapids, Mich.: Zondervan, 1978], p. 124).

Question 7 The following chart might help you compare the attitude Paul describes with the actions Jesus took:

Attitude	Jesus' Actions
"Do nothing out of selfish ambition or vain conceit" (v. 3)	"Who, being in very nature God, did not consider equality with God something to be grasped" (v. 6)
"but in humility" (v. 3)	"he humbled himself and became obedient to death—even death on a cross!" (v. 8)
"consider others better than yourselves" (v. 3)	he "made himself nothing" (v. 7)
"Each of you should look not only to your own interests, but also to the interests of others" (v. 4)	"taking the very nature of a servant" (v. 7)

Question 10 The *NIV Study Bible* explains that "working out your salvation" means: "Work it out to the finish; not a reference to the attempt to earn one's salvation by works, but the expression of one's salvation in spiritual growth and development. Salvation is not merely a gift received once for all; it expresses itself in an ongoing process in which the believer is strenuously involved" (Grand Rapids, Mich.: Zondervan, 1985, p. 1806).

Question 11 "Paul contrasts the life of the believer with the lives of those who live in the world. Unsaved people complain and find fault, but Christians rejoice. Society around us is 'twisted and distorted,' but the Christian stands straight because he measures his life by God's Word, the perfect standard. The world is dark, but Christians shine as bright lights.

The world has nothing to offer, but the Christian holds out the Word of life, the message of salvation through faith in Christ" (Warren W. Wiersbe, *Be Joyful* [Wheaton, Ill.: Victor Books, 1982], p. 63).

STUDY 3
Meekness in Action
MARK 10:32–45; JOHN 13:1–17

Purpose: To learn what Jesus taught about power and to follow his example of serving others with meekness.

Question 2 Though the disciples still had much to learn, they did understand the danger Jesus faced by going to Jerusalem. Because they were Jesus' followers, it was dangerous for them too.

Question 3 The timing of James's and John's request is staggering. Jesus had just described his coming death, yet they failed to understand the impact of the Cross. Their thoughts were still on earthly power and glory.

Question 4 James and John still expected Jesus to establish his messianic kingdom rule on earth, and they wanted to be sure they were prominently involved! They wanted positions of prestige and power and still had a lot to learn about serving with meekness in Jesus' kingdom.

Question 5 It is natural to want God's kingdom and glory now, just as James and John did. We want comfort, security, material possessions, and personal peace—and we don't want to wait for them!

But Jesus and the Scriptures make clear that we must suffer before entering into glory (see Mark 8:31–38; Acts 14:22; 2 Corinthians 4:16–18; 2 Thessalonians 1:5). As one person has said, "The cross comes before the crown." Whenever we seek to avoid suffering for Christ, we end up building our own little kingdom instead of God's.

Question 6 The *cup* "was a Jewish expression that meant to share someone's fate. . . . The cup Jesus had to drink refers to divine punishment of sins that he bore in place of sinful mankind. . . . The image of baptism is parallel to that of the cup, referring to his suffering and death as a baptism" (*NIV Study Bible*, p. 1515).

Question 9 The climax of Jesus' servanthood would be his death on the cross as a ransom for many.

Question 10 Jesus knew of his impending death. He also knew that he possessed all the authority and prestige in the universe (v. 3). Yet in spite of his power and prestige, Jesus was willing to wash his disciples' feet—a task normally performed by a servant or slave. Jesus even knew that Judas would betray him, and yet he served Judas by washing his feet.

Question 11 "Jesus' reply looks beyond the incident to what it symbolizes: Peter needed a spiritual cleansing. The external washing was a picture of cleansing from sin, which Christians also sometimes need" (*NIV Study Bible,* p. 1623).

Question 12 Jesus' teaching grew out of his life and his actions. His teaching about servanthood would probably have had little impact without his powerful example of service. Later, it was probably Jesus' actions more than his words about servanthood that the disciples remembered.

STUDY 4
Meekness Is Not Weakness
2 CORINTHIANS 10:1–11; 12:7–10

Purpose: To understand that meekness is a sign of strength and to learn to be gentle in an evil world.

Question 2 "The Corinthians felt that Paul seemed able to be impressive and strong only at a distance—when he wrote, but not when he appeared or spoke. A saying concerning Paul began to circulate in Corinth: 'His letters are weighty and strong, but his bodily presence is weak, and his speech of no account' (NEB: 'When he appears he has no presence, and as a speaker he is beneath contempt') (II Cor. 10:10).

The personal unimpressiveness of a man supposed to be full of the Spirit was incomprehensible to those who understood the possession of the Spirit to grant power. According to the new Corinthian equation, to be spiritual = to be powerful; and to be weak = to be fleshly. . . . Therefore, Paul, who had acknowledged an evident weakness, was suspected of worldliness or of a lack of authentic spirituality" (Fredrick Dale Bruner, *A Theology of the Holy Spirit* [Grand Rapids, Mich.: Eerdmans, 1970], p. 304).

Question 3 Paul based his appeal on the strong gentleness of Jesus himself. William Barclay describes meekness and gentleness in this way: "It is the quality of the man whose anger is so mastered and so controlled that he is always angry at the right time and never at the wrong time. It describes the man who is never angry at any personal wrong or insult or injury he may receive, but who is capable of righteous anger when he sees others hurt and injured and insulted" (*Letters to Corinthians* [Edinburgh: The Saint Andrew Press, 1973], p. 266).

Questions 4–5 Paul recognized that he was fighting a spiritual battle. The powers of hell were trying to destroy the work of God in Corinth. Paul was prepared for warfare, but his battle weapons would be spiritual, not worldly.

"Paul's attitude of humility was actually one of his strongest weapons, for pride plays right into the hands of Satan. . . . Paul used spiritual weapons to tear down the opposition— prayer, the Word of God, love, the power of the Spirit at work in his life. He did not depend on personality, human abilities, or even the authority he had as an apostle" (Warren W. Wiersbe, *Be Encouraged* [Wheaton, Ill.: Victor Books, 1988], p. 110).

Questions 6–7 "The spiritual leader does not use authority to bring believers to obey the leader. Instead, spiritual authority is always exercised to lead the local body and individual believers to obey Christ. The spiritual leader is not to attempt to exercise control over others; instead, he seeks to free them to be responsive to Jesus" (Lawrence O. Richards, *The Teacher's Commentary* [Wheaton, Ill.: Victor Books, 1987], p. 893).

Question 9 Paul saw his "thorn" as a *gift* from God rather than a punishment from God. This acceptance made it possible for God to accomplish his purposes. The thorn kept Paul from being conceited, and through it he discovered the sufficiency of God's grace.

STUDY 5
Meekness in Ministry
2 TIMOTHY 2:22–26; 1 PETER 5:1–11

Purpose: To learn what it means to minister with meekness and gentleness and to begin practicing servant leadership.

Question 2 "The evil desires of youth" are probably not so much sexual desires, but impatience, arrogance, and self-assertiveness. The opposite of these attitudes is gentleness and meekness.

Question 3 Often we think that being extraordinarily gifted is the most important characteristic for God's servants. But Paul emphasizes holiness, rather than ability, as the most important quality for effectiveness in God's service.

Question 4 "The Lord's servant should not be a fighter but a promoter of unity, by being kind (gentle) to everyone, able or ready to teach those who are willing to learn, and forbearing in the face of differences. . . . He must treat even his opponents with gentle instruction characterized by meekness" (*The Bible Knowledge Commentary* [Wheaton, Ill.: Victor Books, 1983], p. 754).

Question 8 "The elder is not to be a petty tyrant, but to be the shepherd and the example of the flock. . . . There are those who love authority, even if that authority be exercised in a narrow sphere. Milton's Satan thought it better to reign in hell than to serve in heaven. . . . The great characteristic of the shepherd is his selfless care and his sacrificial love for the sheep" (William Barclay, *The Letters of James and Peter* [Edinburgh: The Saint Andrew Press, 1965], p.316).

Question 11 The background for the phrase "clothe yourselves with humility" in verse 5 is interesting. "It comes from a word used of the apron that slaves wore to protect their clothing while at work. Peter would not have forgotten that moment in the Upper Room when Jesus rose from the table, wrapped a towel around his waist, and washed his disciples' feet (John 13:1–15). In the same way, believers are to 'put on the apron of humility to serve one another' (Moffatt). Humility is not a feeling of worthlessness. It is that attitude which allows us to serve one another in ordinary and down-to-earth ways" (Robert H. Mounce, *A Living Hope* [Grand Rapids, Mich.: Eerdmans Publishing Co., 1982], p. 85).

STUDY 6
The Meek Will Inherit
PSALM 37:1–11

Purpose: To recognize the present and future blessings promised to God's meek children and to live as heirs of the King.

Question 4 Is the promise of verse 11 present or future? D. Martyn Lloyd-Jones explains, "The meek already inherit the earth in this life, in this way: A man who is truly meek is a man who is always satisfied, he is a man who is already content. . . . But obviously it has a future reference also" (*Studies in the Sermon on the Mount, Volume I*. [London: Inter-Varsity Press, 1974], p. 71).

Question 5 Psalm 37 teaches perseverance, trust, contentment, and patience in the midst of suffering—a far cry from "name-it-and-claim-it" advocates. David Prior comments, "Endurance and character . . . are seldom the obvious hallmarks of those today who adopt and advocate unrelieved 'prosperity teaching' . . . it produces disciples who reflect the traits of its cultural origins: concentration on instant results; petulance and capitulation when the going is tough; fragility under pressure; an unwillingness if not an outright refusal to look honestly at failure, weakness and sin. . . . In particular, power is seen in terms of getting it, maintaining it and extending it, not in terms of giving, sharing and serving" (*Jesus and Power* [Downers Grove, Ill.: InterVarsity Press, 1987], p. 50).

Question 8 When we worry or fret, our thoughts are focused inward. When we trust, we are focused on God, looking ahead with an eternal perspective. This God-ward view helps us to be meek—to choose the way of patient faith instead of self-assertion.